Pet Needs

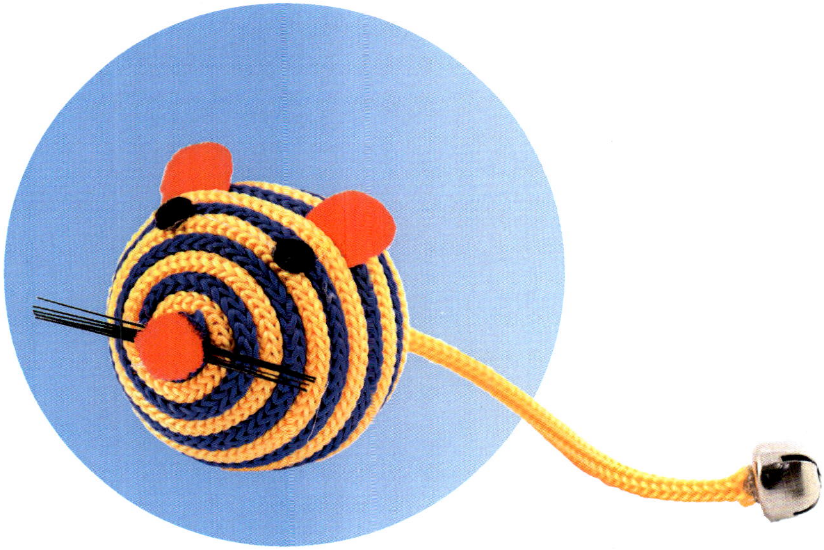

Written by Matthew Holden

macmillan education

My cat needs food.

My cat needs water.

My cat needs a home.

My cat needs a bed.

My cat needs a collar.

My cat needs a toy.

My cat needs a friend.

After Reading

Let's Think About It

- If you had a pet, what do you think it would need?
- How would you look after your pet?
- What would be the best pet for you? Why?

Let's Talk About It

Turn to your partner and discuss your ideas.

- I think a pet would need …
- I would look after my pet by …
- The best pet for me would be … because …

How are your answers the same or different?